A delightful collection
of poetry from British,
American and Australian poets.

Pudmuddle Jump In

Poems selected by
Beverley Mathias
and Jill Bennett

Illustrated by David McKee

A Magnet Book

From Beverley: For Kate and Drew
Louisa too,
And Jacqui who's following on

For Samir from Jill

This anthology first published in Great Britain 1987
by Methuen Children's Books Ltd
This Magnet edition first published 1988
by Methuen Children's Books Ltd
11 New Fetter Lane, London EC4P 4EE
Copyright for this anthology © 1987
by Methuen Children's Books Ltd
Illustrations copyright © 1987 David McKee
Printed in Great Britain
by Cox & Wyman Ltd, Reading

ISBN 0 416 12132 2

Contents

Who's In?

'The door is shut fast
        And everybody's out.'
But people don't know
        What they're talking about!
Say the fly on the wall,
And the flame on the coals,
And the dog on his rug.
And the mice in their holes,
And the kitten curled up,
And the spiders that spin –
'What, everyone out?
        Why, everyone's in!'

Elizabeth Fleming

Caterpillar Walk

High on a leaf,
As happy as could be,
There sat a little caterpillar
Nibbling at a tree.

He went for a walk
With his one, two, three,
A fat little caterpillar
Creeping on a tree.

Clive Sansom

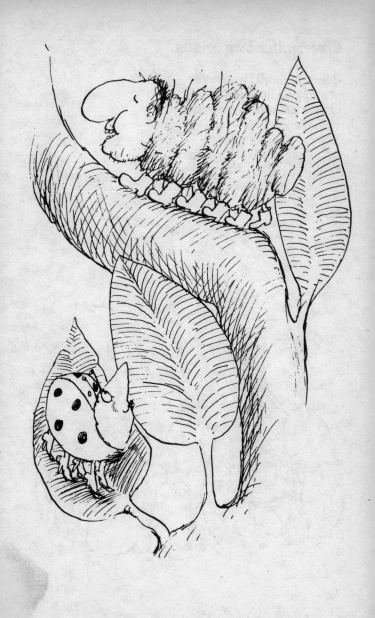

One Snail, Two Snails

One snail and two snails
 Had a little talk;
One snail and two snails
 Went a little walk:
They came to a garden
 And climbed up a tree
Where a jolly old Kookaburra
 Gobbled up the three.

Mary Gilmore

An Introduction To Dogs

The dog is man's best friend.
He has a tail on one end.
Up in front he has teeth.
And four legs underneath.

Dogs like to bark.
They like it best after dark.
They not only frighten prowlers away
But also hold the sandman at bay.

A dog that is indoors
To be let out implores.
You let him out and what then?
He wants back in again.

Dogs display reluctance and wrath
If you try to give them a bath.
They bury bones in hideaways
And half the time they trot sideaways.

They cheer up people who are frowning,
And rescue people who are drowning,
They also track mud on beds,
And chew people's clothes to shreds.

Dogs in the country have fun.
They run and run and run.
But in the city this species
Is dragged around on leashes.

Dogs are upright as a steeple
And much more loyal than people.
Well people may be reprehensibler
But that's probably because they are sensibler.

Ogden Nash

Razor Fish

If you were
to draw
lightly
a straight line
right
down
the margin
of this
sheet of
paper
with your
pen
it wouldn't be
as thin
as a
Razor Fish
seen
edge
ways
on

If you were
to cut
the shape
of a
fish
out of transparent
cellophane
with a
tiny
tail fin
and a mouth
as long

and sharp
as
a
pin
and let it drift
tail up
head down
you wouldn't see –

the Razor Fish
See
what
I
mean?

William Hart-Smith

The Cat's Sleeplessness

By nature's laws
The dog bow-wows,
The ass hee-haws,
Tha cat miaous.
The worst miaous
occur at night,
When cats carouse
With all their might.
A cat miaous
Upon the tiles,
In twenty thousand different styles.

16

In exchange for cream and butter and the other
  things she loots
'Twould be a just and proper thing indeed
To persuade our friend the Pussy to put polish on
  our boots;
And – instead of midnight carolling – to read.

Christine Chagnoux

The Porcupine

Any hound a porcupine nudges
Can't be blamed for harbouring grudges.
I know one hound that laughed all winter
At a porcupine that sat on a splinter.

Ogden Nash

Tadpoles

Ten little tadpoles
    playing in a pool.
'Come,' said the water-rat,
    'come along to school.
Come and say your tables,
    sitting in a row.'
And all the little tadpoles said,
    'No, no, no!'

Ten little tadpoles
    swimming in and out,
Racing and diving
    and turning round about.
'Come,' said their mother,
    'dinner-time, I guess.'
And all the little tadpoles cried,
    'Yes, yes, yes!'

Rose Fyleman

The Derby Ram

As I was going to Derby upon a market day,
I met the finest ram, sir, that ever fed on hay,
       On hay, on hay, on hay,
I met the finest ram, sir, that ever fed on hay.

This ram was fat behind, sir,
       this ram was fat before,
This ram was ten yards round, sir,
       indeed he was no more,

No more, no more, no more,
This ram was ten yards round, sir,
indeed he was no more.

The horns grew on his head, sir,
they were so wondrous high,
As I've been plainly told, sir,
they reached up to the sky,
The sky, the sky, the sky,
As I've been plainly told, sir,
they reached up to the sky.

The tail grew on his back, sir,
was six yards and an ell,
And it was sent to Derby to toll the market bell,
The bell, the bell, the bell,
And it was sent to Derby to toll the market bell.

Traditional

The Caterpillar

Brown and furry
Caterpillar in a hurry;
Take your walk
To the shady leaf or stalk.

May no toad spy you,
May the little birds pass by you;
Spin and die,
To live again a butterfly.

Christina Georgina Rossetti

Song 20

How doth the little busy bee
    Improve each shining hour,
And gather honey all the day
    From every opening flower!

How skilfully she builds her cell!
    How neat she spreads the wax!
And labours hard to store it well
    With the sweet food she makes.

In works of labour or of skill
    I would be busy too:
For Satan finds some mischief still
    For idle hands to do.

In books, or work, or healthful play
    Let my first years be past,
That I may give for every day
    Some good account at last.

Isaac Watts

The Duck

Behold the duck.
It does not cluck.
A cluck it lacks.
It quacks.
It is especially fond
Of a puddle or a pond.
When it dines or sups,
It bottom ups.

Ogden Nash

Shepherd's Night Count

One ewe,
One ram,
Two sheep,
One lamb,
Three sheep,
One flock,
Four gates,
One lock,
Five folds,
One light,
Good dog,
Good night.

Jane Yolen

Another True Story

There was a little rabbit sprig,
Who being little, was not big;
He always walked upon his feet,
And never fasted when he eat.
When from a place he ran away,
He never at that place did stay;
And when he ran, as I am told,
He ne'er stood still for young or old.
Though ne'er instructed by a cat,
He knew a mouse was not a rat:
One day, as I am certified,
He took a whim and fairly died;
And, as I'm told by men of sense,
He never has been walking since.

Traditional

The Search

I went to find a pot of gold
That's waiting where the rainbow ends.
I searched and searched and searched and
    searched
And searched and searched, and then –
There it was, deep in the grass,
Under an old and twisty bough.
It's mine, it's mine, It's mine at last . . .
What do I search for now?

Shel Silverstein

The Troll Bridge

This is the Bridge
of the
Terrible Troll.
No one goes
by
without paying
a toll,
a terrible toll
to the Troll.

It's no place to
loll, to
linger or
stroll.
to sing or to
play.

So if ever you
ride
to the
opposite side,
be ready to
pay
the terrible troll –
I mean terrible toll –
to the Terrible Toll –
I mean Troll.

Lilian Moore

Full of the Moon

It's full of the moon
The dogs dance out
Through brush and bush and bramble.
They howl and yowl
And growl and prowl.
They amble, ramble, scramble.
They rush through brush.
They push through bush.
They yip and yap and hurr.
They lark around and bark around
With prickles in their fur.
They two-step in the meadow.
They polka on the lawn.
Tonight's the night
The dogs dance out
And chase their tails till dawn.

Karla Kuskin

The Little Elf

I met a little Elf-man, once,
    Down where the lilies blow.
I asked him why he was so small,
    And why he didn't grow.

He slightly frowned, and with his eye
    He looked me through and through.
'I'm quite as big for me,' said he,
    'As you are big for you.'

John Kendrick Bangs

The Firefly

This beast is real, but fabulous;
    An animated spark,
It weaves soft patterns through the night
    And punctuates the dark;

A firework that is soundless,
    By no crude taper lit;
A flame that you can handle –
    If you can capture it.

Edward Lowbury

A Moon-Witch

A moon-witch is no joke.
She comes in a sort of smoke.
She wisps in through the keyhole and feels about
Like a spider's arm or a smoke-elephant's snout
Till she finds her victim.
He collapses like a balloon – she has sucked him
Empty in a flash. Her misty feeler
Blooms red as blood in water, then milkily paler –
And fades. And a hundred miles off
She disguises her burp with a laugh.

Also she has a sort of electronic
Rocket-homing trick – and that is chronic.
She steals the signature
Of whoever she wants to bewitch
And swallows it. Now wherever he might be
He sees her face, horrible with evil glee,
Hurtling at him like a rocket – WHOP!
People see him stop.

He staggers, he smooths his brow,
    he is astonished –
Whatever it was, it seems to have vanished.

He doesn't know what he's in for.
He's done for.

Only deep in sleep he dreams and groans
A pack of hyenas are fighting over his bones.

In a week, he dies. Then 'Goodness!'
    the witch says,
And yawns and falls asleep for about ten days –
Like a huge serpent that just ate
Something its own weight.

Ted Hughes

The Fairies

Up the airy mountain,
    Down the rushy glen,
We daren't go a-hunting
    For fear of little men;
Wee folk, good folk,
    Trooping all together;
Green jacket, red cap,
    And white owl's feather.

Down along the rocky shore
    Some make their home,
They live on crispy pancakes
    Of yellow tide-foam;
Some in the reeds
    Of the black mountain lake,
With frogs for their watch-dogs,
    All night awake.

William Allingham
(*first two stanzas only*)

The Secret Song

Who saw the petals
    drop from the rose?
I, said the spider,
But nobody knows.

Who saw the sunset
    flash on the bird?
I, said the fish,
But nobody heard.

Who saw the fog
    come over the sea?
I, said the pigeon,
Only me.

Who saw the first
    green light of the sun?
I, said the night owl,
The only one.

Who saw the moss
    creep over the stone?
I, said the grey fox,
All alone.

Margaret Wise Brown

London Wall

A Roman built up London Wall,
    With his big bricks and his little bricks
A Roman built up London Wall
With its straw and its lime and its mortar and all.

Then he stood on the top, so stalwart and tall,
    On the big bricks and the little bricks,
He stood on the top so stalwart and tall,
With his spear and his shield
            and his helmet and all.

He looked down on London, all bustle and brawl
    And big bricks and little bricks,
He looked down on London, all bustle and brawl,
With its streets and its chimneys
            and markets and all.

With its mansions, its rivers,
       its parks and Whitehall,
   And its big bricks and its little bricks,
With its mansions, its rivers,
       its parks and Whitehall,
Its prisons, its churches, its Tower and St. Paul.

'I've built up a Wall that never can fall,
    With my big bricks and my little bricks,
I've built up a Wall that never can fall
By cannon, or thunder, or earthquake and all!'

But London laughed low and began for to crawl
    Through the big bricks and the little bricks,
London laughed low and began for to crawl
To the North, to the West, to the South,
      East and all.

There came a great crack in the side of the Wall,
    In the big bricks and the little bricks,
There came a great crack in the side of the Wall,
And down fell the Wall and the Roman and all!

Eleanor Farjeon

The Witches' Ride

Over the hills
Where the edge of the light
Deepens and darkens
To ebony night,
Narrow hats high
Above yellow bead eyes,
The tatter-haired witches
Ride through the skies.
Over the seas
Where the flat fishes sleep
Wrapped in the slap of the slippery deep,
Over the peaks
Where the black trees are bare,
Where bony birds quiver
They glide through the air.
Silently humming
A horrible tune,
They sweep through the stillness
To sit on the moon.

Karla Kuskin

Eeka, Neeka

Eeka, Neeka, Leeka, Lee –
Here's a lock without a key;
Bring a lantern bring a candle,
Here's a door without a handle;
Shine, shine, you old thief Moon,
Here's a door without a room;
Not a whisper, moth or mouse,
Key – lock – door – room: where's the house?

Say nothing, creep away,
And live to knock another day!

Walter de la Mare

I'm Nobody! Who are you?

I'm Nobody! Who are you?
Are you – Nobody – Too?
Then there's a pair of us?
Don't tell! they'd advertise – you know!

How dreary – to be – Somebody!
How public – like a Frog –
To tell one's name – the livelong June –
To an admiring Bog!

Emily Dickinson

Growing

When I grow up I'll be so kind,
Not yelling 'Now' or 'Do you MIND!'
    Or making what is called a scene,
    Like 'So you're back' or 'Where've you BEEN.'
Or 'Goodness, child, what is it NOW?'
Or saying 'STOP . . .that awful row',
    Or 'There's a time and place to eat'
    And 'Wipe your nose' or 'Wipe your feet'.
I'll just let people go their way
And have an extra hour for play.
    No angry shouting 'NOW what's wrong?'
    It's just that growing takes so long.

Max Fatchen

Sulk

I scuff
      my feet along
And puff
      my lower lip
I sip my milk
      in slurps
And huff
And frown
And stamp around
And tip my chair
      back from the table
Nearly fall down
      But I don't care
I scuff
And puff
And frown
And huff
And stamp
And pout
Till I forget
What it's about

Felice Holman

Tarantulas

I don't mind about tarantulas, do you?
I don't care
If they stare
From my picture-frames
Or roof.
I'm aloof
To the fact
They are very large
And act
As if they might
Quite conceivably
Bite.
I find
If they *know*
You don't mind,
They are quiet as a mouse;
Unobtrusive in the house;
Helpful with flies;
Friendly and wise –

So,
I don't mind about tarantulas, do you?

Mary King

Lies

When we are bored
My friend and I
Tell
Lies.

It's a competition: the prize
Is won by the one
Whose lies
Are the bigger size.

We really do:
That's true.
But there isn't a prize:
That's lies.

Kit Wright

Laundromat

You'll find me in the Laundromat – just me and
    shirts and stuff:
Pyjamas, pillowcases, socks and handkerchiefs
    enough.
I've put them in my special tub – the third one
    from the right,
And set the switch for *Warm*, and shoved the coin
    and got the light,
And sprinkled blue detergent on the water pouring
    in,
Closed down the lid and bought a Coke to watch
    the shakes begin
To travel up the line of empty units. How they
    show
Their pleasure just to feel one fellow full and on
    the go!
Well, now it's all one train: a nice long rumbly
    kind of freight,
Of which I am the engineer. We're running on the
    straight,
In Diesel Number Three I've got the throttle open
    wide,
And blow for every crossing through the pleasant
    countryside.
The light turns amber. Pretty soon some other
    washers bring
Their bulgy bags of clothes and make tubs nine
    and seven sing.
But nine and seven haven't got the squiggle,
    squash and drive
Of Number Three. May sound alike to you but I'm
    alive

To certain water music that the third one seems to
    make.
I hear it change from rinse to spin, and now it
    doesn't shake.
Green light! The spin is over, the longer job is
    done;
And what was washed is plastered to the walls
    from being spun.
You'd think the tub is empty, since the bottom's
    clear and bright;
I'm glad the spinning earth can't throw *us* out into
    the night!
For that is where we'd go, because the sky is not a
    wall;
But earth's content to hold us with our dirty shirts
    and all.
Still, spinning *is* a funny thing: the tub goes like a
    top.
The dryer, on the other hand, runs like a wheel. I
    plop
The damp unsorted pillowcases, hanks, and socks,
    and what
Into a kind of squirrel cage, that generates a lot
Of heat when set at *Medium*. But this one needs
    the dime
I haven't got! I'll dry some other clothes some
    other time.

David McCord

John and Jim

I've got a secret friend
Who lives at home with me.
Even when we're talking
There's no one there to see.
    My name's John and his name's Jim.
    You can see me, but you can't see him.

I've got a secret friend
Who goes to school with me.
Even when we're walking
There's no one there to see.
    My name's John and his name's Jim.
    You can see me, but you can't see him.

I've got a secret friend
Who sits in class with me.
Even when we're writing
There's no one there to see.
    My name's John and his name's Jim.
    You can see me, but you can't see him.

I've got a secret friend
Who likes to box with me.
Even when we're fighting
There's no one there to see.
    My name's John and his name's Jim.
    You can see me, but you can't see him.

Barbara Ireson and Christopher Rowe

It's Dark Outside

It's dark outside.
It's dark inside.
It's dark behind the door.

I wonder
if I'm brave enough
to walk across the floor.

I am –
at least I think I am.
I'll try it once and see
if Mum comes up
or stays downstairs
with Dad and cups of tea.

Nancy Chambers

Every Time I Climb a Tree

Every time I climb a tree
Every time I climb a tree
Every time I climb a tree
I scrape a leg
Or skin a knee
And every time I climb a tree
I find some ants
or dodge a bee
And get the ants
All over me.

And every time I climb a tree
Where have you been?
They say to me
But don't they know that I am free
Every time I climb a tree?
I like it best
To spot a nest
That has an egg
Or maybe three.

And then I skin
The other leg
But every time I climb a tree
I see a lot of things to see
Swallows rooftops and TV
And all the fields and farms there be
Every time I climb a tree.
Though climbing may be good for ants
It isn't awfully good for pants
But still it's pretty good for me
Every time I climb a tree.

David McCord

I'm Really Not Lazy

I'm really not lazy –
I'm not!
I'm not!
It's just that I'm thinking
And thinking
And thinking
A lot!
It's true I don't work
But I can't!
I just can't!
When I'm thinking
And thinking
And thinking
A lot!

Arnold Spilka

T-Shirt

T-shirt
you're my best thing
though you've faded so much
no one knows what you said when you
were new.

Myra Cohn Livingston

Thinking

Silently
Inside my head
Behind my eyes
A thought begins to grow and be
A part of me.
And then I think
I always knew
The thing I only got to know,
As though it always
Was right there
Inside my head
Behind my eyes
Where I keep things.

Felice Holman

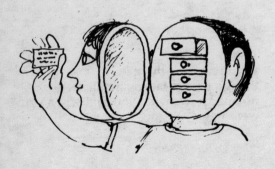

Far Away

How far, today,
Is far away?
It's farther now than I can say,
It's farther now than you can say,
It's farther now than who can say,
It's very *very* far away:
You'd better better better play,
You'd better stay and play today.
Okay . . . okay . . . okay.

David McCord

What a Day

What a day,
Oh what a day.
My baby brother ran away,
And now my tuba will not play.
I'm eight years old
And turning grey,
Oh what a day,
Oh what a day.

Shel Silverstein

Weather

Dot a dot dot dot a dot dot
Spotting the windowpane.
Spack a spack speck flick a flack fleck
Freckling the windowpane.

A spatter a scatter a wet cat a clatter
A splatter a rumble outside.
Umbrella umbrella umbrella umbrella
Bumbershoot barrel of rain.

Slosh a galosh slosh a galosh
Slither and slather a glide
A puddle a jump a puddle a jump
A puddle a pump aluddle a dump a
Puddmuddle jump in and slide!

Eve Merriam

in Just –

in Just –
spring   when the world is mud –
luscious the little
lame balloonman

Whistles   far   and wee

and eddieandbill come
running from marbles and
piracies and it's
spring

when the world is puddle-wonderful

the queer
old balloonman whistles
far   and   wee
and betyandisbel come dancing

from hop-scotch and jump-rope and

it's
spring
and
    the

          goat-footed

balloonMan   whistles
far
and
wee

e e cummings

June

The day is warm
and a breeze is blowing,
the sky is blue
and its eye is glowing,
and everything's new
and green and growing . . . .

My shoes are off
and my socks are showing . . . .

My socks are off. . . .

Do you know how I'm going?

                BAREFOOT!

Aileen Fisher

In the Sun

Sit
on your doorstep
or any place.

Sit
in the sun
and lift your face.

Close your eyes and
sun dream.
Soon the warm warm sun
will seem
to fill you up
and
spill over.

Lilian Moore

Autumn Leaves

Down
   down
      down
Red
   yellow
      brown
Autumn leaves tumble down,
Autumn leaves crumble down,
Autumn leaves bumble down,
Flaking and shaking,
Tumbledown leaves.

Skittery
Flittery
Rustle by
Hustle by
Crackle and crunch
In a snappety bunch.

Run and catch
Run and snatch
Butterfly leaves
Sailboat leaves
Windstorm leaves.
Can you catch them?

Swoop.
Scoop,
Pile them up
On a stompy pile and
Jump
       Jump
          JUMP!

Eve Merriam

Puddles

There are large puddles, small puddles,
All made by the rain,
Brown puddles, black puddles,
Puddles in the lane,
Puddles we step over,
Puddles we jump through,
Cold puddles, warm puddles,
Muddy puddles, too.

There are puddles by the wayside,
Puddles in the field,
Puddles gaily shining
Like a soldier's glinting shield.
Puddles that go splash,
Puddles that go splosh.
Puddles here so deep
We need a mackintosh.

J Stickells

Mallee in October

When clear October suns unfold
mallee tips of red and gold,

children on their way to school
discover tadpoles in a pool,

iceplants sheathed in beaded glass,
spider orchids and shivery grass,

webs with globes of dew alight
budgerigars on their first flight,

tottery lambs and a stilty foal,
a papery slough that a snake shed whole,

and a bronzewing's nest of twigs so few
that both the sky and the eggs show through.

Flexmore Hudson

December Leaves

The fallen leaves are cornflakes
That fill the lawn's wide dish,
And night and noon
The wind's a spoon
That stirs them with a swish.

The sky's a silver sifter
A-sifting white and slow,
That gently shakes
On crisp brown flakes
The sugar known as snow.

Kaye Starbird

70

Listen, I'll Tell You

Listen, I'll tell you
a wonderful thing:
there was an old woman
made wholly of string!
Her legs and her arms
and her petticoat too,
her fingers and stockings,
the lace in her shoe,
and even her hair –
which was longer than mine –
were made from a tenpenny
bundle of twine.
Now, do you not think it
delightful to sing
of this tweisty old woman
made wholly of string?

Jean Kenward

Things

Trains are for going,
Boats are for rowing,
Seeds are for sowing,
Noses for blowing,
    And sleeping's for bed.

Dogs are for pawing.
Logs are for sawing,
Crows are for cawing,
Rivers for thawing,
    And sleeping's for bed.

Flags are for flying,
Stores are for buying,
Glasses for spying,
Babies for crying,
    And sleeping's for bed.

Cows are for mooing,
Chickens for shooing,
Blue is for bluing,
Things are for doing,
    And sleeping's for bed.

Games are for playing,
Hay is for haying,
Horses for neighing,
Saying's for saying,
    And sleeping's for bed.

Money's for spending,
Patients for tending,
Branches for bending;
Poems for ending,
    And sleeping's for bed.

William Jay Smith

Sandy Sawyer

Strawberries grow for Sandy Sawyer
When other people's plants have none;
His peas are greener and more tender,
And his potatoes, every one,
Have such a smiling sort of look
As if it pleased them all to be
In Sandy's patch of garden ground
Between the pasture and the sea.
Even the trees in his orchard bend
With twists and knots in every limb,
As if they tried with might and main
To make themselves look just like him.

Rachel Field

74

Riddle

Allow me to describe myself.
       I live upon a dusty shelf,
With other sorts who do the same.
       I have a title to my name,
Yet wear a jacket without sleeves.
I'm not a plant, but I have leaves.
       (It's also true I'm not a tree,
Though that is what *I used* to be.)
I'm full of words, but cannot speak,
       I sometimes vanish for a week,
and then return to my dear nook.
You've guessed it – I'm a library book!

Colin West

Breakdown

Rackerty clackerty
clickerty BONG
the washing machine
has gone terribly wrong,

It's swallowed a button!
It's stuck in its jaw!
Do you think it will ever
get out any more?

Hark at it spluttering
clickerty-bump –
the washing is churning
all up in a lump.

And just for a button
so shiny and small!
O why did we ever
have buttons at all?

Rackerty clackerty
clickerty clack . . .
Hooray! THAT sounds better –
the button's come back!

Jean Kenward

Blackfriars

By the shot tower
    near the chimneys
Off the road to
    Waterloo
Stands the cottage
    of 'The Ancient'
As in eighteen-
    forty two.
Over brickwork,
    brownish brickwork
Lilac hangs in
    London sun
And by light fan-
    tastic clockwork
Moves the drawbridge
    sounds the gun.

When the sunset
    in the side streets
Brought the breezes
    up the tide
Floated bits of
    daily journals
Stable smells and
    silverside.
And the gaslight
    yellow gaslight
Flaring in its
    wiry cage,
Like the Prison
    Scene in *Norval*
On the old Ol-
    ympic stage,
Lit the archway
    as the thunder
And the rumble
    and the roll
Heralded a
    little handcart
And 'The Ancient'
    selling coal.

John Betjeman

Australian Windmill Song

By the clay-red creek on the dry summer day,
    With never a trickle or pool,
An old windmill stands with a racketing wheel
    And it sings of the water that's cool.

And the sheep hear its song
        on the long, dusty plains
    While the rusty tank leaks at its seams
And the old windmill sings of the far-away rains
    And the grass of the sheep farmer's dreams.

The scummy trough stands
      where the thirsty sheep come
   And the magpies and crows dip their beaks,
While the wind on the wheel
      with its summer breath drums
   And the whirlwinds will dance past the creeks.

But the old windmill goes
      with a wheeze and a clank
   With the sun beating down on its tower
As it lifts up the water to flow in the tank
   While the sheep farmer longs for a shower.

The night's full of stars
      and the moon's bright and low
   As it climbs from the ranges nearby
And the soft-muzzled 'roos to the water trough go
   By the tank that must never run dry.

The farmer will smile at the racket and thump,
   Then he sleeps for he's lulled by the sound
As the windmill draws life
      with the pulse of its pump
   From the sweet, hidden streams underground.

Max Fatchen

Magical Eraser

She wouldn't believe
This pencil has
A magical eraser.
She said I was a silly moo,
She said I was a liar too,
She dared me prove that it was true,
And so what could I do –
I erased her!

Shel Silverstein

The Engineer

Let it rain!
Who cares?
I've a train
Upstairs,
With a brake
Which I make
From a string
Sort of thing,
Which works
In jerks
'Cos it drops
In the spring,
Which stops
With the string,
And the wheels
All stick
So quick
That it feels
Like a thing
That you make
With a brake,
Not string . . . .

So that's what I make,
When the day's all wet.
It's a good sort of brake
But it hasn't worked yet.

A A Milne

I like to see it lap the Miles

I like to see it lap the Miles –
And lick the Valleys up –
And stop to feed itself at Tanks –
And then – prodigious step

Around a Pile of Mountains –
And supercilious peer
In Shanties – by the sides of Roads –
And then a Quarry pare

To fit its Ribs
And crawl between
Complaining all the while
In horrid – hooting stanza –
Then chase itself down Hill

And neigh like Boanerges –
Then – punctual as a Star
Stop – docile and omnipotent
At its own stable door –

Emily Dickinson

The Sailor

I'd like to be a sailor – a sailor bold and bluff –
Calling out 'Ship ahoy!' in manly tones and gruff.
I'd learn to box the compass,
  and to reef and tack and luff;
I'd sniff and sniff the briny breeze
  and never get enough.
Perhaps I'd chew tobacco,
  or an old black pipe I'd puff;
   But I wouldn't be a sailor if . . .
    The sea was very rough.
     Would you?

C J Dennis

Miss T.

It's a very odd thing –
    As odd as can be –
That whatever Miss T. eats
    Turns into Miss T.;
Porridge and apples,
    Mince, muffins and mutton,
Jam, junket, jumbles –
    Not a rap, not a button
It matters; the moment
    They're out of her plate,
Though shared by Miss Mutcher
    And sour Miss Bate;
Tiny and cheerful,
    As neat as can be,
Whatever Miss T. eats
    Turns into Miss T.

Walter de la Mare

Daniel
inscribed to Isador Bennett Reed

(Beginning with a strain of 'Dixie')
Darius the Mede was a king and a wonder,
His eye was proud, and his voice was thunder.
He kept bad lions in a monstrous den.
He fed up lions on Christian men.

(With a touch of 'Alexander's Ragtime Band')
Daniel was the chief hired man of the land.
He stirred up the music in the palace band.
He whitewashed the cellar. He shovelled in
    the coal.
And Daniel kept a-praying: – 'Lord save my soul.'
Daniel kept a-praying: – 'Lord save my soul.'
Daniel kept a-praying: – 'Lord save my soul.'

Daniel was the butler, swagger and swell.
He ran upstairs. He answered the bell.
And *he* would let in whoever came a-calling: –
Saints so holy, scamps so appalling.
'Old man Ahab leaves his card.
Elisha and the bears are a-waiting in the yard.
Here comes Pharoah and his snakes a-calling.
Here comes Cain and his wife a-calling.
Shadrach, Meschach and Abednego for tea.
Here comes Jonah and the whale,
And the *Sea!*
Here comes St Peter and his fishing pole.
Here comes Judas and his silver a-calling.
Here comes old Beelzebub a-calling.'
And Daniel kept a-praying: – 'Lord save my soul.'
Daniel kept a-praying: – 'Lord save my soul.'
Daniel kept a-praying: – 'Lord save my soul.'

His sweetheart and his mother were Christian
      and meek.
They washed and ironed for Darius every week.
One Thursday he met them at the door: –
Paid them as usual, but acted sore.

He said: – 'Your Daniel is a dead little pigeon.
He's a good hard worker, but he talks religion.'
And he showed them Daniel in the lion's cage.
Daniel standing quietly, the lions in a rage.
His good old mother cried: –
'Lord save him.'
And Daniel's tender sweetheart cried: –
'Lord save him.'

(This to be repeated three times, very softly and slowly)
And she was a golden lily in the dew.
And she was as sweet as an apple on the tree
And she was as fine as a melon in the corn-field,
Gliding and lovely as a ship on the sea,
Gliding and lovely as a ship on the sea.

And she prayed to the Lord: –
'Send Gabriel, Send Gabriel.'

King Darius said to the lions: –
'Bite Daniel, Bite Daniel.
Bite him. Bite him. Bite him!'

(Here the audience roars with the leader)
Thus roared the lions: –
'We want Daniel, Daniel, Daniel,
We want Daniel, Daniel, Daniel.
Grrrrrrrrrrrrrrrrrrrrrrrrrrrrrrrrrrrrrrrrrrrrrrrrr
Grrrrrrrrrrrrrrrrrrrrrrrrrrrrrrrrrrrrrrrrrrrrrrrrr.'

(The audience sings this with the leader, to the old Negro tune)
And Daniel did not frown.
Daniel did not cry.
He kept on looking at the sky.
And the Lord said to Gabriel: –
'Go chain the lions down,
Go chain the lions down,
Go chain the lions down,
Go chain the lions down.'

And Gabriel chained the lions,
And Gabriel chained the lions,
And Gabriel chained the lions,

And Daniel got out of the den,
And Daniel got out of the den,
And Daniel got out of the den.
And Darius said: – 'You're a Christian child,'
Darius said: – 'You're a Christian child,'
Darius said: – 'You're a Christian child,'

And gave him his job again,
And gave him his job again,
And gave him his job again.

Vachel Lindsay

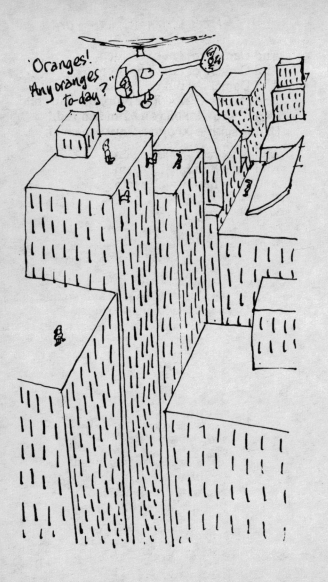

Street Cries of New York

Pineapples

'Pine Apples! Fine flavored Pine Apples!'

Here's ripe Pine Apples,
    Well flavored and sound,
Come buy one or two,
    Very good they'll be found.

New milk

'Meeleck, Come! Meeleck, Come!'

Here's New Milk from the Cow,
    Which is so nice and so fine,
That the doctors do say,
    It is much better than wine.

Oranges

'Any Oranges today?'

Here's fine sweet Oranges,
    Rich flowing with juice,
Just arrived from abroad,
    Ripe and ready for use.

Traditional

Australia

Quite obviously in Australia
Everything's upside down;
And you must be an absolute failure
If you happen to wear a crown.

Do you walk, to get through a door,
On the ceiling? Does a bird
Perch out of harm on the floor?
Is 'top' a rather rude word?

Is headball played and elevennis?
If you hate anyone is it love?
Of course, they don't know where heaven is
Except that it's not up above.

Are holidays longer than terms?
Are humbugs good for you?
No doubt deep in the sky are worms,
And served first is last in the queue.

Do dogs sniff each other's noses
And wag them when they are glad?
Are dandelions not roses
Carefully grown by Dad?

Do children go to the office?
Does Mother tell awful lies?
And Grandpa buy comics and toffees,
Gran's skirt give her chilly thighs?

If so, I'll not go to Australia,
Where at jokes a listener sobs.
Besides, I prefer a dahlia
To grow flowers rather than knobs.

Roy Fuller

Laughing Time

It was laughing time, and the tall giraffe
Lifted his head, and began to laugh:

Ha! Ha! Ha! Ha!

And the Chimpanzee on the ginko tree
Swung merrily down with a *Tee Hee Hee:*

Hee! Hee! Hee! Hee!

'It's certainly not against the law!'
Croaked Justice Crow with a loud guffaw:

Haw! Haw! Haw! Haw!

The dancing Bear who could never say 'No'
Waltzed up and down on the tip of his toe:

Ho! Ho! Ho! Ho!

The Donkey daintily took his paw,
And around they went: Hee-Haw! Hee-Haw!

Hee-Haw! Hee-Haw!

The moon had to smile as it started to climb;
All over the world it was laughing time!

Ho! Ho! Ho! Ho! Hee-Haw! Hee-Haw!

Hee! Hee! Hee! Hee! Ha! Ha! Ha! Ha!

William Jay Smith

Ping-Pong

Chitchat
wigwag
rick rack
zigzag

Knickknack
geegaw
riffraff
seesaw

crisscross
flip-flop
ding-dong
tiptop

singsong
mishmash
King Kong
        bong.

Eve Merriam

97

Frog

A frog once went out walking,
In the pleasant summer air,
He happened into a barber's shop
And skipped into the chair.
The barber said in disbelief;
'Your brains are surely bare.
How can you have a haircut.
When you haven't any hair'.

Traditional

98

Have You . . .

Have you ever, ever, ever
In your long legged life
Seen a long legged sailor
With a long legged wife?
No, I've never, never, never
In my long legged life
Seen a long legged sailor
With a long legged wife.
. . . a short legged life . . .
. . . a cross-eyed life . . .
. . . and elbow life . . .
. . . a knee-cap life . . .
. . . an ankle life . . .
. . . a nosey life . . .

Traditional clapping rhyme

Mummy Slept Late and Daddy Fixed the Breakfast

Daddy fixed the breakfast.
He made us each a waffle.
It looked like gravel pudding.
It tasted something awful.

'Ha, ha,' he said, 'I'll try again.
This time I'll get it right.'
But what *I* got was in between
Bituminous and anthracite.

'A little too well done? Oh well,
I'll have to start all over.'
That time what landed on my plate
Looked like a manhole cover.

I tried to cut it with a fork:
The fork gave off a spark.
I tried a knife and twisted it
Into a question mark.

I tried it with a hack-saw.
I tried it with a torch.
It didn't even make a dent.
It didn't even scorch.

The next time Dad gets breakfast
When Mummy's sleeping late,
I think I'll skip the waffles.
I'd sooner eat the plate!

John Ciardi

Eletelephony

Once there was an elephant,
Who tried to use the telephant –
No! No! I mean an elephone
Who tried to use the telephone –
(Dear me! I am not certain quite
That even now I've got it right.)

Howe'er it was, he got his trunk
Entangled in the telephunk;
The more he tried to get it free,
The louder buzzed the telephee –
(I fear I'd better drop the song
Of elephop and telephong!)

Laura E Richards

The Man From Menindee

The Man from Menindee was counting sheep:
He counted so hard that he went to sleep.
    He counted by threes
    And he counted by twos,
    The rams and the lambs
    And the wethers and ewes.
He counted six thousand three hundred and ten
And when he woke up he'd to count them again.

D H Soutar

Song of the Train

Clickety-clack,
Wheels on the track,
This is the way
They begin the attack:
Click-ety-clack,
Click-ety, *clack*-ety,
Click-ety
Clack.

Clickety-clack,
Over the crack,
Faster and faster
The song of the track:
Clickety-clack,
Clickety-clack
Clickety, clackety,
Clackety
Clack.

Riding in front,
Riding in back,
Everyone hears
The song of the track:
Clickety-clack,
Clickety-clack,
Clickety, *clickety*,
Clackety
Clack.

David McCord

Riddles 1 and 2

Four stiff-standers,
Four dilly-danders,
Two lookers,
Two crookers,
And a wig-wag

A cow

In marble walls as white as milk,
Lined with a skin as soft as silk;
Within a fountain crystal clear,
A golden apple doth appear.
No doors there are to this stronghold,
Yet thieves break in and steal the gold.

Traditional

An egg

Pennies From Heaven

I put 10p in my Piggy Bank
To save for a rainy day.
It rained the *very next morning*!
Three cheers, Hip Hip Hooray!

Spike Milligan

King's Cross

King's Cross!
what shall we do?
His Purple Robe
Is rent in two!
Out of his crown
He's torn the gems!
He's thrown his Sceptre
Into the Thames!
The Court is shaking
In its shoe –
King's Cross!
What shall we do?
Leave him alone
For a minute or two.

Eleanor Farjeon

Song of the Pop-Bottlers

Pop bottles pop-bottles
    In pop shops;
The pop-bottles Pop bottles
    Poor Pop drops.

When Pop drops pop-bottles,
    Pop-bottles plop!
Pop-bottle-tops topple!
    Pop mops slop!

Stop! Pop'll drop bottle!
    Stop, Pop, stop!
When Pop bottles pop-bottles,
    Pop-bottles pop!

Morris Bishop

On the Ning Nang Nong

On the Ning Nang Nong
Where the Cows go Bong!
And the Monkeys all say Boo!
There's a Nong Nang Ning
Where the trees go Ping!
And the teapots Jibber Jabber Joo.
On the Nong Ning Nang
All the mice go Clang!
And you just can't catch 'em when they do!
So it's Ning Nang Nong!
Cows go Bong!
Nong Nang Ning!
Trees go Ping!
Nong Ning Nang!
The mice go Clang!
What a noisy place to belong,
Is the Ning Nang Ning Nang Nong!!

Spike Milligan

As I Went Down Zig Zag

As I went down Zig Zag
    The clock striking one,
I saw a man cooking
    An egg in the sun.

As I went down Zig Zag
    The clock striking two,
I watched a man walk
    With one boot and one shoe.

As I went down Zig Zag
    The clock striking three,
I heard a man murmuring
    'Buzz!' like a bee.

As I went down Zig Zag
    The clock striking four,
I saw a man swim
    In no sea by no shore.

As I went down Zig Zag
    The clock striking five,
I caught a man keeping
    A hog in a hive.

As I went down Zig Zag
    The clock striking six,
I met a man making
    A blanket of bricks.

As I went down Zig Zag
    The clock striking seven,
A man asked me if
    I was odd or was even.

As I went down Zig Zag
    The clock striking eight,
I saw a man sailing
    A seven-barred gate.

As I went down Zig Zag
    The clock striking nine,
I saw man milking
    Where never were kine.

As I went down Zig Zag
    The clock striking ten,
I saw a man waltzing
    With a cock and a hen.

As I went down Zig Zag
    The clock striking eleven,
I saw a man baking
    A loaf with no leaven.

As I went down Zig Zag
    The clock striking twelve,
For dyes from the rainbow
    I saw a man delve.

So if you'd keep your senses,
    The point of my rhyme
Is don't go down Zig Zag
    When the clocks start to chime.

Charles Causley

Ethel Read a Book

Ethel read,
Ethel read,
Ethel read a book.
Ethel read a book in bed,
She read a book on Ethelred.
The book that Ethel read in bed,
(The book on Ethelred) was red.
The book was red that Ethel read,
In bed on Ethelred.

Colin West

Poor Old Penelope

Poor old Penelope,
great are her woes,
a pumpkin has started
to grow from her nose.
'My goodness,' she warbles,
'this makes me so glum,
I'm perfectly certain
I planted a plum.'

Poor old Penelope,
wet are her tears,
two pigeons are perched
on the lobes of her ears.
'How dreadful,' she moans,
'I've such terrible luck.
I'd hoped for a goose
and a dear little duck.'

Poor old Penelope.
sad is her tale,
this morning an elephant
reached her by mail.
'Oh bother,' she mutters,
'I fear that I'm sunk
for all that I sent for
was one little trunk.'

Jack Prelutsky

Well Bread

If you cast your bread on the waters,
It returns a thousand fold,
So it says in the Bible,
That's what I've been told.

(So) I cast my bread on the waters,
It was spotted by a froggy,
And the bits of bread *he* didn't eat
Just floated back all soggy.

Spike Milligan

Spaghetti! Spaghetti!

Spaghetti! spaghetti!
you're wonderful stuff,
I love you, spaghetti,
I can't get enough.
You're covered with sauce
and you're sprinkled with cheese,
spaghetti! spaghetti!
oh, give me some please.

Spaghetti! spaghetti!
piled high in a mound,
you wiggle, you wriggle,
you squiggle around.
There's slurpy spaghetti
all over my plate,
spaghetti! spaghetti!
I think you are great.

Spaghetti! spaghetti!
I love you a lot,
you're slishy, you're sloshy,
delicious and hot.
I gobble you down
oh, I can't get enough
spaghetti! spaghetti!
you're wonderful stuff.

Jack Prelutsky

Mr. Mistoffelees

You ought to know Mr. Mistoffelees!
The Original Conjuring Cat –
(There can be no doubt about that).
Please listen to me and don't scoff. All his
Inventions are off his own bat.
There's no such Cat in the metropolis;
He holds all the patent monopolies
For performing surprising illusions
And creating eccentric confusions.
  At prestidigitation
    And at legerdemain
  He'll defy examination
    And deceive you again.
The greatest magicians have something to learn
From Mr. Mistoffelees' Conjuring Turn.
Presto!
  Away we go!
    And we all say: OH!
      Well I never!
      Was there ever
      A Cat so clever
        As Magical Mr. Mistoffelees!

He is quiet and small, he is black
From his ears to the tip of his tail;
He can creep through the tiniest crack,
He can walk on the narrowest rail.
He can pick any card from a pack,
He is equally cunning with dice;
He is always deceiving you into believing
That he's only hunting for mice.
  He can play any trick with a cork
    Or a spoon and a bit of fish-paste;

If you look for a knife or a fork
    And you think it is merely misplaced –
You have seen it one moment, and then it is *gawn*!
But you'll find it next week lying out on the lawn.
    And we all say: OH!
      Well I never!
      Was there ever
      A Cat so clever
        As Magical Mr. Mistoffelees!

His manner is vague and aloof,
You would think there was nobody shyer –
But his voice has been heard on the roof
When he was curled up by the fire.
And he's sometimes been heard by the fire
When he was about on the roof –
(At least we all *heard* that somebody purred)
Which is incontestable proof
    Of his singular magical powers:
      And I have known the family to call
    Him in from the garden for hours,
      'While he was asleep in the hall.

And not long ago this phenomenal Cat
Produced *seven kittens* right out of a hat!
    And we all said: OH!
      Well I never!
      Did you ever
      Know a Cat so clever
        As Magical Mr. Mistoffelees!

T S Eliot

Old Hogan's Goat

Old Hogan's goat
Was feeling fine,
He ate a red shirt
Right off the line.

I took a stick
And beat his back,
And tied him to
A railway track.

A speeding train
Was drawing nigh,
Old Hogan's goat
Was doomed to die.

He gave an aw-
ful shriek of pain,
Coughed up that shirt
And flagged that train.

Traditional

120

Not So Gorgeous

Dorothy's drawers are creamy gauze;
  Lil's are long and slack;
Tonia's tights are crocheted whites;
  Jennifer Jane's are black.

Betty's bloomers are slaty grey,
  And she tucks her skirt inside;
Polly's are pink – since yesterday –
  I think she's had them dyed.

Sarah's silks were awf'ly dear –
  The best her mum could get;
And (may I whisper it in your ear?)
  Nancy's knickers are wet!

Sue's are blue, and Prue's are too,
  And little Pam's are sweet;
While naughty Meg has lost a leg,
  And Tilly has torn her seat.

Swanky Maisie's are trimmed with daisies
  And patched with coloured stuffs;
But those on Milly look awful silly –
  They sort of flap their cuffs!

Jill's have frills, and Pat's are plain,
  With a button in case they fall;
And (may I whisper once again?)
  I haven't a pair at all!

J A Lindon

Aunt Samantha

Aunt Samantha woke one day
and sat up in her bed,
when a middle-sized rhinoceros
sat squarely on her head.

She did not seem the least put out,
was not at all annoyed;
in fact, as she addressed the beast,
she sounded overjoyed.

'I'm very glad you're up there,
though you've squashed my head quite flat,
for you've saved me all the botherment
of putting on my hat.'

Jack Prelutsky

Index of Poets

Acknowledgements

Jack Prelutsky, 'Poor Old Penelope', 'Aunt Samantha' from *The Queen of Eene*, by Jack Prelutsky, Copyright © 1970, 1978 by Jack Prelutsky. 'Spaghetti! Spaghetti!' from *Rainy Rainy Saturday*, by Jack Prelutsky. Copyright © 1980 by Jack Prelutsky. Reprinted with the permission of Greenwillow Books (A Division of William Morrow & Company).

William Jay Smith, 'Laughing Time' and 'Things' from *Nonsense Poems* by William Jay Smith, published by Delacorte Press, 1980. Copyright © 1955, 1957, 1980 by William Jay Smith. Reprinted by permission of William Jay Smith.

Max Fatchen, 'Growing', 'Australian Windmill Song' from *Songs For My Dog and Other People* by Max Fatchen (Kestrel Books, 1980), pp 18, 60–61. Copyright © 1980 by Max Fatchen. Reproduced by permission of Penguin Books Ltd.

Nancy Chambers, 'It's dark outside . . .' from *Stickleback, Stickleback and Other Minnow Rhymes* by Nancy Chambers (Kestrel Books, 1971), Copyright © Nancy Chambers, 1977. Reproduced by permission of Penguin Books Ltd.

Ted Hughes, 'A Moon-Witch' from *Moon-Bells and Other Poems* by Ted Hughes. Reprinted by permission of Faber and Faber Ltd.

Edward Lowbury, 'The Firefly'. Reprinted with the permission of the author.

Jean Kenward, 'Listen, I'll Tell You' from *Old Mister Hotchpotch* and 'Breakdown'. Reprinted by permission of the author.

Walter de la Mare, 'Eeka, Neeka' and 'Miss T'. Reprinted with the permission of The Literary Trustees of Walter de la Mare and The Society of Authors as their representative.

Emily Dickinson, 'I like to see it lap the Miles'. Reprinted by permission of the publishers from *The Poems of Emily Dickinson*, Thomas H. Johnson, ed., Cambridge, Mass.: Harvard University Press, Copyright 1951, © 1955, 1979, 1983 by the President and Fellows of Harvard College.

A. A. Milne, 'The Engineer' from *Now We Are Six*. Reprinted by permission of Methuen Children's Books.

John Betjeman, 'Blackfriars'. Reprinted by permission of John Murray (Publishers) Ltd.

J. A. Lindon, 'Not So Gorgeous'. Reprinted with the permission of Frank R. Lindon.